JUNIOR ■ WORLD ■ BIOGRAPHIES

Rachel Carson

JAKE GOLDBERG

D0150780

CHELSEA JUNIORS

a division of CHELSEA HOUSE PUBLISHERS

Chelsea House Publishers
EDITOR-IN-CHIEF: Remmel Nunn
MANAGING EDITOR: Karyn Gullen Browne
COPY CHIEF: Juliann Barbato
PICTURE EDITOR: Adrian G. Allen
ART DIRECTOR: Maria Epes
DEPUTY COPY CHIEF: Mark Rifkin
ASSISTANT ART DIRECTOR: Noreen Romano
MANUFACTURING MANAGER: Gerald Levine
SYSTEMS MANAGER: Lindsey Ottman
PRODUCTION MANAGER: Joseph Romano
PRODUCTION COORDINATOR: Marie Claire Cebrián

JUNIOR WORLD BIOGRAPHIES

EDITOR: Remmel Nunn

Staff for RACHEL CARSON
PICTURE RESEARCHERS: Susan Biederman, Jonathan Shapiro
SENIOR DESIGNER: Marjorie Zaum
COVER ILLUSTRATOR: Michael Garland

3 5 7 9 8 6 4 2

Library of Congress Cataloging-in-Publication Data
Goldberg, Jake.
    Rachel Carson/Jake Goldberg.
        p. cm.—(Junior world biographies)
    Summary: Describes the life of the conservationist, known for her work in
protecting the environment.
    ISBN 0-7910-1566-1
    1. Carson, Rachel, 1907–64—Juvenile literature.
    2. Ecologists—United States—Biography—Juvenile literature.
    [1. Carson, Rachel, 1907–64.   2. Conservationists.
    3. Biologists.]
    I. Title. II. Series.
QH31.C33G64   1991
574'.092—dc20   90-49342
[B]   CIP
[92]   AC

Rachel Carson

Contents

Young Rachel grew up on her parent's farm in Springdale, Pennsylvania, north of Pittsburgh.

1

A Farm Girl from Pennsylvania

Rachel Carson was a biologist, a writer, and one of the first environmental activists of modern times. She was also a woman courageously fighting for a place in a man's world. Both her life and her books have inspired many young people, especially women, to dedicate themselves to careers in science. Her special love of the sea gave many of her readers their first look at life in this mysterious world. People of all ages first learned of threats to the environment from her writings. She was one of the first people to teach that human beings were a part of nature, not separate from it. She also warned that if people were not careful they could destroy nature and themselves.

Rachel Louise Carson was born on May 27, 1907, in Springdale, Pennsylvania, a town eleven miles north of Pittsburgh. Her father, Robert Carson, was a farmer and a businessman. Her mother, Maria, a very independent-minded woman, was a teacher. Her parents had been married in 1894 and moved to Springdale in 1900.

Rachel was the youngest of three children. She had a brother, Robert, Jr., who was eight years older than she, and a sister, Marian, who was ten years older. The family lived on a small farm on a hill above the Allegheny River. They were not rich. They made a little money selling apples from their orchard, and at different times in his life Rachel's father tried to sell land and insurance. But this had not worked out, and the family just managed to make ends meet. The family members were always very close to one another, and all her life Rachel was especially close to her mother.

When she was still very young, Rachel worked on the farm. She would milk the cows, feed the pigs, and gather the hens' eggs. She would play with the family's dog, cats, and rabbits. She learned how to make butter and cheese from milk. She planted a garden near the house. She helped pick the apples and vegetables at harvest time. Her mother would often take her for long walks in the woods, where Rachel was delighted to study the plants and birds. She developed a deep respect for nature. She learned the names and habits of the plants, birds, and insects in the forests near the farm.

With the city of Pittsburgh so close, Rachel's farm was in the middle of coal and steel country. Rachel saw what industry could do to the land. The blast furnaces that made the nation's steel belched black smoke into the air. Heaps of slag, the burned waste from the furnaces, were piled all over the countryside. The Allegheny

Rachel sits on her mother's lap, between her sister, Marian, and her brother, Robert, Jr.

River, which the Indians had called the "beautiful river," was choked with barges carrying coal and steel and had become polluted. At one time a coal company wanted to dig a mine shaft right under the Carsons' farm, but the Carsons refused to grant them permission. The Carsons loved the land and did not want to see it spoiled. From the very beginning of her life, Rachel was made to see the beauty and value of the natural world around her.

The early years of the twentieth century were the time of the suffragettes, women who wanted the right to vote, which women did not have before 1920. Rachel's mother admired the goals of the women's movement and encouraged her daughter to develop her mind. She taught Rachel not to be afraid to be interested in things even if others said they were the wrong subjects for women to study. She encouraged her to choose friends who shared her interests and to not just try to become popular with everybody. Rachel's mother was very protective and believed that her daughter had special abilities that would become obvious as she grew up. Rachel became a quiet girl who loved to read, write, and draw pictures. Because she had scarlet fever when she was very young, she was never a strong child. But she was curious, studied hard, and did very well in school.

In 1917, when Rachel was only ten years old, the United States went to war with Germany. Thousands of young American men were drafted into the army and sent to fight in Europe. Rachel's parents were patriotic, but they were very worried about the suffering the war would cause. They were also disturbed by the prejudice many people showed toward German Americans. War seemed to bring out the worst feelings in people. The Carsons talked about these problems with their children.

Rachel's older brother, Robert, joined the U.S. Army Aviation Service. The letters he wrote to his sister from Europe excited her, and when she was still only in the fourth grade she wrote a very imaginative story about a heroic Canadian

*Rachel's brother served in the U.S. Army Aviation
Service during World War I. At home on leave, he
told stories of the war that inspired Rachel to write.*

pilot. The story was called "A Battle in the Clouds," and it was soon published in a popular magazine. Many people praised the story, and Rachel got her first taste of what it might be like to write for a living. She later wrote, "Perhaps that early experience of seeing my work in print played its part in fostering my childhood dream of becoming a writer."

Rachel wrote more stories about soldiers and the war, but the war ended in 1918. Rachel was growing up, and her interests were changing. She became interested in nature and wildlife. She also read everything she could find about the sea, even though the farm where she grew up was hundreds of miles from the nearest seacoast and Rachel had never seen the ocean. Though they sparked her curiosity, the nature books available to Rachel were not very good.

At the time, nature writers were very different from what they are today. Most writers of nature books tried to make animals behave like human beings and gave them human virtues such as kindness and courage. But a few people, such as former president Theodore Roosevelt, an early leader of the conservation movement, argued that this was wrong and that writers should describe nature "like it is." Life was not always pretty. It could be a harsh struggle for survival. Rachel was influenced by this new way of thinking and began to read more realistic writers. Later on she would adopt this more realistic style in her own books.

More than anything else, though, Rachel was interested in the sea. So little was known about life in the oceans at this time. Oceanography was a new field, and even a farm girl from Pennsylvania might have a chance to make a few discoveries. "I was fascinated by the ocean although I had never seen it," she later wrote. "I dreamed of it and I longed to see it, and I read all the sea literature I could find."

Life in the sea always fascinated Rachel Carson, even though she did not get her first look at an ocean until after graduating college.

2

The Lure
of the Sea

In 1925, Rachel Carson left home to attend Pennsylvania College for Women (now named Chatham College) in Pittsburgh. Rachel lived away from home in a dormitory. On weekends she would go home or her mother would come to visit her. At college she soon learned that many of her fellow students were less interested in scholarship than in partying. This era was called the Roaring Twenties, and many young people, weary of the war years and their hardships, just wanted to have a good time. But Rachel was a serious student. She worked for the college newspaper, joined the literary club, and wrote stories and poems for the college literary magazine. Her secret desire was to become a writer. The American writer she most admired at the time was Mark Twain. "His philosophy, humor, and straightforward hatred of hypocrisy," she wrote in an essay, "have touched a responsive chord in my heart."

In her second year at college, Rachel took a course in biology and became very interested in the subject. She enjoyed the field trips to study the rivers and forests of western Pennsylvania. She also liked working in the laboratory, studying living things under the microscope. The love of nature she acquired as a young girl on her parents' farm now took on the discipline of science. The more she came to understand how nature really worked, the more the natural world fascinated her. Her biology teacher, Mary Scott Skinker, was an important influence on her life, and Rachel and Mary became good friends.

Rachel decided to switch her major from English to biology. At the time, this was a very brave decision. Society was still very prejudiced against educated and independent women, and almost nobody wanted to hire a woman scientist. Many of her friends and teachers tried to discourage her. They believed that if she studied biology, she would never find a job in a man's world. If she studied English, there were at least some famous woman writers, and she could always get a job as a teacher. But Rachel was very determined. She was considered one of the school's best students, and so friends and teachers helped her as much as they could. Some even gave her small sums of money to help her stay in school.

In 1929, Rachel Carson graduated with high honors. She had done so well that she received a full scholarship for advanced study at Johns Hopkins University in Baltimore, Maryland.

Before going to graduate school, Carson

The Woods Hole Marine Biological Laboratory on Cape Cod, Massachusetts

got a summer job at the Woods Hole Marine Biological Laboratory on Cape Cod in Massachusetts. Now known as the Woods Hole Oceanographic Institute, it has always been one of the most important centers for ocean research in the United States. For Carson this was a very important summer. The boat ride from New York City across Long Island Sound to Woods Hole was the first time in her life that she had actually seen the ocean. At Woods Hole she worked in a laboratory dissecting fish, but there was plenty of time to walk along the seashore to study the tides and watch the shorebirds. She would examine all the little creatures she found in the pools of water among the rocks. Carson had read about these creatures in books, but now she could examine them with her own eyes. This was a very exciting time for her. She enjoyed working with the other scientists at Woods Hole, and she came to understand that her destiny would be to study the sea.

Just before beginning her graduate studies at Johns Hopkins in Baltimore, Carson went to Washington, D.C., to speak to Elmer Higgins, who was head of scientific research at the U.S. Bureau of Fisheries. She had heard that Higgins was a good person who tried to encourage young scientists. Higgins liked Carson but told her honestly what her other friends had told her: It would be very hard for a woman to find a job as a scientist. But he promised to try to help her after she finished graduate school.

Carson began her graduate studies in Baltimore in 1929 just as the Great Depression hit the United States. Millions of people lost their jobs as factories and businesses closed. It was a very discouraging time to be studying for an advanced science degree, knowing that there would probably be no jobs waiting when she finished. To save money, Carson's parents left their Pennsylvania farm and moved into her small, rented cottage a short trolley ride from Johns Hopkins University. Though Carson had a scholarship, she tried to earn extra money by teaching during the summers.

Carson graduated in 1932 with a master's degree in marine zoology, but there were very few jobs for anybody, let alone a woman scientist. In 1933 her brother, Robert, Jr., lost his job and moved in with Rachel and her parents. He found work repairing radios, but there was not much money in it. Then in 1935 her father died. It was a very difficult and sad time for the whole family.

Soon, however, things began to change for the better, not only for Carson but for all Americans. A new president had come into the White House, Franklin Delano Roosevelt. He took a new approach to dealing with the depression by starting programs designed to create jobs. Carson was encouraged to see that Roosevelt had appointed a woman, Frances Perkins, to be secretary of labor. This was the first time in the history of the United States that a woman had held a cabinet post. And the president's wife, Eleanor Roosevelt, was becoming a public figure herself, speaking out on behalf of women's rights and other issues. Maybe it was getting a little bit easier to compete in a man's world.

Elmer Higgins, head of scientific research at the U.S. Bureau of Fisheries, gave Rachel Carson her first writing assignment in 1935.

Studying living creatures under the microscope was a joy to Rachel Carson throughout her life.

3

Success
as a Writer

In her search for work, Rachel Carson traveled to Washington, D.C. She again called on Elmer Higgins at the U.S. Bureau of Fisheries. Higgins made good on his promise to help and hired her to write the scripts for a weekly radio show about life in the ocean called "Romance Under the Waters." On his staff, Higgins either had writers who did not know enough science or scientists who were not skilled writers. Carson wrote later, "I think at that point he was having to write the scripts himself. He talked to me a few minutes and then said: 'I've never seen a written word of yours, but I'm going to take a sporting chance.'" In Rachel Carson he found a woman who was a trained scientist and a skilled writer. She was perfect for the job. Everyone liked her work, and Carson was thrilled with the assignment.

Carson wrote three radio scripts and was paid $19.25 for each one. The writing was so good that Higgins hired her as a part-time writer for $1,000 a year. This salary was low in those days (it would be less than $10,000 today), but the job allowed Carson to combine her two favorite activities: writing and studying the sea. This, she decided, was what she really wanted to do with her life.

Carson took the civil service examination for a full-time government job and earned the highest score that had ever been attained. She thus became a full-time employee of the U.S. Bureau of Fisheries—only the second woman ever hired by the bureau—and she worked in Higgins's office. Her job title was to be junior aquatic biologist. Tremendously excited, she moved from Baltimore to Silver Spring, Maryland, to be closer to her new Washington office. Unfortunately, just at this time Rachel's older sister, Marian, died, and Rachel had to take in Marian's two young daughters. Her mother helped her care for the two children.

One of the articles Carson wrote at this time was so good that Higgins told her to send it to the *Atlantic Monthly,* one of the best-known literary magazines in the country. In 1937 the magazine published her article "Undersea," and she received dozens of letters from people who enjoyed it. Carson began to feel that the risks she had taken in studying science were beginning to pay off. "It dawned on me that by becoming a biologist I had given myself something to write about."

Hendrik Willem van Loon, a popular writer of the day, also read Carson's article and felt that she had a special ability to explain life in the sea to people who wanted to know more about it. Van Loon went to his publishing company, Simon & Schuster, and spoke to his editor there, Quincy Howe. Howe met with Carson and asked her to write a book about undersea life.

Carson worked for three years at night and on weekends. "My constant companions during those otherwise solitary sessions were two precious Persian cats, Buzzie and Kito. Buzzie in particular used to sleep on my writing table, on the litter of notes and manuscript sheets." Her first book, *Under the Sea-Wind*, was finally published in 1941. Her purpose, she wrote, was to "make the sea and its life as vivid a reality for those who may read the book as it has become for me during the past decade."

Under the Sea-Wind is made up of stories in which the main characters are creatures of the sea. One story is about a family of shorebirds that must fly north to their nesting site in the Arctic. Another story is about a mackerel that tries to reach its spawning ground before it is eaten by other fish. In all the stories, Carson tried to draw a true picture of life in the sea. She tried to show that life was a constant struggle for survival. She argued that life and death are part of a great cycle in which living things depend on each other for food. She did not try to make life in the sea seem prettier or easier than it really was. For this reason, many people consider her to be one of the first modern nature writers.

Of all her writings, Rachel Carson always thought of *Under the Sea-Wind* as her favorite book. "I have been so pleased," she wrote, "with the reception the purely scientific people, who so often have little patience with popularizations of science, have given the book." It was widely praised, but it did not sell very well. Just as it was published, the Japanese attacked Pearl Harbor, and the United States was at war again. All Americans were caught up in the struggle for victory. The depression was forgotten, and personal careers did not seem so important any more. Of the book's appearance, Carson later wrote, "The world received the event with superb indifference."

During the war, Carson was very busy. The U.S. Bureau of Fisheries, where she worked, had become part of the U.S. Fish and Wildlife Service. Carson helped prepare information on ocean currents and depths, which was used to make more accurate ocean charts. The charts were of great value to the army and the navy in their struggle against the Germans and the Japanese. Ships and submarines depended on these charts. She also produced pamphlets that urged Americans to eat more fish so that meat could be conserved for the soldiers who were fighting in other countries. In this way, Carson became an important and valued member of the agency.

Working for the government during wartime was exhausting, and Carson wanted more time to devote to her own writing. She applied for jobs at the New York Zoological Society, the National Audubon Society, and *Reader's Digest* (a popular magazine), but there was still much

*Rachel Carson with her diving equipment
off the Florida coast*

prejudice against the idea of a woman scientist, so Carson stayed at her government post. She became editor in chief of all Fish and Wildlife Service publications. She described the work she did in a letter: "My job consists of general direction of the publishing program of the Service— working with authors in planning and writing their manuscripts, reviewing manuscripts submitted, and overseeing the actual editing and preparation of the manuscripts for the printer. I have a staff of six assistants who handle the various details of this sort, including planning or executing illustrations, selecting appropriate type faces, plannings, general page layouts and design. It is really just the work of a small publishing house."

When she was not working, Carson spent much of her free time at home with her mother and her nieces. She also joined a local chapter of the Audubon Society and went for early morning walks through the parks of Washington to look at birds. Though she was a quiet person, she made friends among her fellow workers easily and was remembered by them with affection. A co-worker said that Carson's "zest and humor made even the dull stretches of bureaucratic procedure a matter for quiet fun, and she could instill a sense of adventure into the editorial routine of a government department."

Though she was very busy, Carson did manage to continue writing. One of the most interesting articles she wrote during the war years, published in 1944 in *Reader's Digest*, was "The Bat Knew It First." This article told the story of radar and how bats used sound waves to locate objects in the dark long before scientists had figured out how to do it with radio waves.

In the years right after the war, still working as editor in chief of publications for the U.S. Fish and Wildlife Service, Carson helped publish a series of twelve booklets called "Conservation in Action." The purpose was to encourage the spirit of conservation among the American people. In her introduction to the series, she wrote, "Wild creatures, like men, must have a place to live. As civilization creates cities, builds highways, and drains marshes, it takes away, little by little, the land that is suitable for wildlife. As their spaces for living dwindle, the wildlife populations themselves decline." In order to prepare these pamphlets, Carson was permitted to travel to various nature reserves around the country. She traveled up and down the Atlantic coast and even as far as Oregon. "Of course I'd like to spend all my time doing just that sort of thing," she wrote to a friend, "but our budget is not likely to permit very much of it."

During these same years, Carson also began to write her second book, in which she hoped to describe all the new scientific discoveries that were made about the oceans during the war years. She wanted it to be the kind of book that ordinary people could understand without scientific training, but she wanted it to be scientifically accurate. "I am impressed by man's dependence upon the ocean, directly, and in thousands of ways unsuspected by most people," she told a friend. "These relationships, and my belief that we will become even more dependent upon the ocean as we destroy the land, are really the themes of this book."

Carson began writing in 1948, but the work went slowly. A well-known ocean scientist and admirer of Carson's writings, Dr. William Beebe, told her, "You can't write this book until you have gotten your head underwater." Dr. Beebe had been the first person to descend into the deep ocean in a *bathysphere*, a steel diving sphere with windows for deep-sea observation. So in 1949, Carson put on a diver's helmet and went under the ocean to explore the coral reefs off the Florida Keys. For the first time she saw for herself what she described as the "misty green vistas of a strange, nonhuman world."

Later that same year Carson also joined the crew of the *Albatross III*, a research ship belonging to the U.S. Fish and Wildlife Service, as they cruised the waters of the North Atlantic studying the ocean. The main purpose of the voyage was to study population changes among several fish species favored by commercial fishermen. Carson watched the crew haul in their nets carrying many kinds of fish, which she would examine under a microscope in the ship's

Dr. William Beebe, the renowned ocean scientist who advised Rachel Carson to go underwater before she wrote The Sea Around Us

laboratory. These adventures helped her understand the ocean better and made it easier for her to finish her writing.

Carson's second book, *The Sea Around Us*, was finally finished in 1950. It told the story of the oceans from prehistoric times to the present and talked about tides and currents, plants and fish, and the different ways human beings have used the ocean. It was beautifully written. Parts of it first appeared in the pages of several magazines—the *Yale Review*, *Science Digest*, *Vogue*, and the *New Yorker*. One of these chapters earned an award from the American Association for the Advancement of Science. They called Carson's work the "finest example of science writing in any American magazine in 1950." The complete book first appeared in 1951.

The Sea Around Us was an instant success. It appeared on the list of best-selling books in the *New York Times* and stayed on that list for more than twenty months. It was translated into thirty-two different languages around the world. The book received many awards, including the John

Burroughs Medal given to nature books of high literary merit. Rachel Carson received many honorary degrees from colleges and universities. In England, she was elected a Fellow of the Royal Society of Literature. In the United States, she was elected to the National Institute of Arts and Letters, becoming the second woman to share this honor.

The Sea Around Us received the National Book Award for the best nonfiction book of 1951. Upon receiving this award, Carson modestly said, "If there is poetry in my book about the sea, it is not because I put it there but because no one could write truthfully about the sea and leave out the poetry." Carson always belittled her own talents. She once said, "The discipline of the writer is to learn to be still and listen to what his subject has to tell him."

The Sea Around Us was so successful that her publishers decided to reissue her first book, *Under the Sea-Wind*, which had not done well because World War II had turned people's attention in another direction. As a result, in 1952, Rachel Carson had *two* books on the best-seller list. Though she was pleased that people enjoyed her writing, she was not comfortable with all the attention she began to receive and continued to try to live as privately as possible.

Hollywood made a movie based on *The Sea Around Us*. Carson felt that the movie was not well made and not scientifically accurate, and she vowed never to let anyone make a movie from her writings unless she had more control over the script. All the same, the movie won an Academy Award for best full-length documentary of 1953. The name of this modest farm girl, who had not seen the ocean until after graduating from college, was becoming more widely known in the United States. When the famous orchestra conductor Arturo Toscanini recorded Claude Debussy's *La Mer* (The Sea), Carson herself was asked to write the notes for the back of the record album.

Rachel Carson would often search for unusual creatures in the tidal pools near her cottage in Maine.

CHAPTER

4

A New Cause

The success of *The Sea Around Us* gave Rachel Carson financial security. She was able to leave her job with the U.S. Fish and Wildlife Service. She bought some land on the coast of Maine near the town of West Southport and built a cottage there. Life was easier now. Carson could do whatever she wanted to do, and these next few years were happy ones. She would often walk along the shore, listening to the sound of the waves beating against the rocks. Sometimes she would take tiny creatures from pools of water among the rocks and bring them back to her cottage. Here she would examine them with her microscope. But she was always careful not to harm these creatures, and she would always put them back into the water afterward.

Her studies of the Maine coast gave Carson the idea for her next book, *The Edge of the Sea*. The subject of this book was life where the oceans and the land come together. In it she described this seashore world as the "primeval meeting place of the elements of earth and water, a place of compromise and conflict and eternal change." Carson wrote about the Atlantic coast of North America, from the jagged, rocky shoreline of Maine, where she lived, to the tidal wetlands and coral reefs of Florida. She wrote about how the coastlines were formed millions of years ago, and what life is like there today. She described the life of plants and animals that live part of the time underwater and part of the time in open air. She wrote about crabs and shrimps, barnacles and sponges, and starfish and snails. Their lives are governed by the waves and the tides, and they must be able to survive on land as well as in the sea. Because their world is so different from that of the deep sea, they look and behave differently from fish and other creatures that stay underwater and swim all day.

Earlier, in *Under the Sea-Wind* Carson had written about the attraction of the seashore. "To stand at the edge of the sea, to sense the ebb and the flow of the tides, to feel the breath of a mist moving over a great salt marsh, to watch the flight of shorebirds that have swept up and down the surf lines of the continents for untold thousands of years, to see the running of the old eels and the young shad to the sea, is to have knowledge of things that are as nearly eternal as any earthly life can be."

The Edge of the Sea was published in 1955 and also became a best-seller. Rachel Carson became even more well known. In 1956 she wrote another short book, *The Sense of Wonder*, to help young people understand and appreciate nature. Throughout her life, Carson devoted a lot of time to educating children. She took in and raised the sons and daughters of brothers and sisters who had died, and she understood just how special the child's view of things was. "A child's world is fresh and new and beautiful, full of wonder and excitement," she wrote. "It is our misfortune that for most of us that clear-eyed vision, that true instinct for what is beautiful and awe-inspiring, is dimmed and even lost before we reach adulthood."

Rachel Carson was now at the height of her career. She no longer had to worry about money, and she was living quietly and comfortably right next to her beloved ocean. But she was beginning to notice things about the way people treated nature that made her less optimistic about the future. In the years after the war, it appeared to her that some politicians were trying to stop conservation programs. These politicians wanted to give the nation's forests and parklands back to the lumber and mining companies.

Like many other people, Carson was also very worried about the growing number of nuclear weapons in the world. After the war, the government tried to promote the peaceful use of nuclear power, but all the world could see the dangers of this new form of energy from the two atom bombs that had been dropped on Japan. And many more atomic weapons were being exploded during tests in the deserts of the southwestern United States. Scientists were beginning to speak about the long-term dangers of atomic radiation.

This was also the time of the "cold war," when the United States and the Soviet Union became very suspicious of each other. Because of this cold war, many people—scientists and concerned citizens—who disagreed with the politicians were called disloyal. The new president, Dwight D. Eisenhower, appointed Douglas McKay secretary of the interior. McKay had called people interested in preserving the environment "long-haired punks." The government began to dismiss from its ranks scientists and others who did not agree with the new policies. Carson was angry enough about these dismissals to send a letter to the *Washington Post* in which she wrote, "It is one of the ironies of our time that, while concentrating on the defense of our country against enemies from without, we should be so heedless of those who would destroy it from within."

All these things disturbed Rachel Carson very much. It seemed to her that for the first time in history, human beings were powerful enough to change nature, and they were doing this in alarming ways. A new world war with atomic weapons was unthinkable. And new industries were changing the face of the land. She decided that the next book she wrote would be about problems with the environment. Instead of describing nature with beautiful words and earning the praise of readers, Carson felt that she would now have to point the finger of blame at many irresponsible people and risk their anger.

In the late 1950s, Carson found the subject for her next book. To kill mosquitoes, the state

A U.S. Department of Agriculture C-47 cargo airplane was capable of spraying DDT over vast areas of virgin forest.

of Massachusetts had sprayed the chemical DDT onto a salt marsh along the Atlantic coast near the small town of Duxbury. An old friend of Carson's, Olga Owens Huckins, had established a bird sanctuary nearby. Huckins noticed not only that not all of the mosquitoes were killed but that many birds, bees, and other creatures had died after the spraying.

Huckins wrote to Carson to protest what DDT was doing to wildlife in the area. This was not the first time that Carson had heard about the side effects of insect-killing chemicals. When she had worked for the government, she had read many similar reports. Around the world, pesticides had done much good by killing off disease-carrying and crop-eating insects. But they also destroyed many plants, small animals, and other useful insects. And nobody seemed to know whether or not these chemicals could harm human beings.

What made Carson especially angry was that the government and the chemical companies seemed to be working together to ignore or block anyone who complained. For Carson, the use of DDT became a symbol for the destruction of the environment and all the powerful but indifferent people who were allowing this destruction to take place. "The more I learned about the use of pesticides," she wrote later, "the more appalled I became. I realized that here was the material for a book. What I discovered was that everything which meant the most to me as a naturalist was being threatened, and that nothing I could do would be more important."

Carson also understood how much more difficult it would be to tell this story. It was not simply a matter of writing well or of proving to anyone that a woman could be a good scientist. Now she would enter the arena of politics and special interests, and she was sure to be attacked and personally criticized.

Rachel Carson always wrote slowly and carefully, and the result was some of the most beautiful nature writing in the English language.

5

Silent Spring

Personal and family problems prevented Rachel Carson from writing as much or as quickly as she wanted to. In 1957 her niece Marjorie died, and Rachel had to take in and care for Marjorie's five-year-old son. The next year her ninety-year-old mother also passed away. This was a big blow, because Rachel and her mother had been very close all their lives. They had lived together since the 1930s, and more important, Rachel's mother had always been the one to encourage and support her in whatever she tried to do. Carson wrote of her mother, "She could fight fiercely against anything she believed wrong, as in our present Crusade! Knowing how she felt about that will help me to return to it soon, and to carry it through to completion."

And as if that was not enough, in 1960, Rachel Carson learned that she had breast cancer. There was grim humor in this because her own research was beginning to show that many cancers might be caused by the poisonous chemicals people were putting into the land, water, and air. The radiation treatments she received left her weak and disheartened, but she continued with her writing.

In researching her book, Carson read hundreds of scientific papers and contacted scientists from all over the world. She spoke to her former boss, Elmer Higgins, who had also reported on the dangers of pesticides. She discovered that government researchers knew full well that these chemicals were dangerous, but their superiors were not allowing them to speak out.

The government and the chemical industry were working hand in hand to make sure that the harmful effects of these chemicals were kept hidden.

Carson worked hard, and finally in 1962 the first parts of her new book, called *Silent Spring*, appeared in the *New Yorker* magazine. The complete book was published later that same year. The title for *Silent Spring* was chosen because Carson began her book with a fable. What would happen to a typical American town if everyone woke up one spring morning to find that all the birds and tiny animals had died? "On the mornings that had once throbbed with the dawn chorus of robins, catbirds, doves, jays, wrens and scores of other bird voices," she wrote, "there was now no sound; only silence lay over the fields and woods and marsh." Unlike her earlier books, *Silent Spring* was not to be a celebration but a warning: "This imagined tragedy may easily become a stark reality we all shall know."

In the book, Carson described the great power that modern science had given human beings to change the world. It had taken most living creatures millions of years to adapt to their habitats. They could not possibly adapt to and survive the rapid changes human beings could now bring about with their knowledge of science and chemistry. The chemicals human beings made were not natural, and nature had no defense against them. Therefore human beings had to act responsibly and carefully whenever they used their knowledge to change nature.

Carson also suggested that the damage done by pesticides and toxic chemicals might not stop with just birds and tiny creatures. She gave an example of a field of alfalfa that had been sprayed with DDT. Cows would eat the alfalfa, and some of the DDT would get into the cows' milk, and then people would drink the milk. If this happened often enough, many people would soon have large amounts of DDT in their bodies. At the time that Carson wrote her book, scientists were still not sure how serious DDT contamination could be. But it is now known that cancer, birth defects, and other serious diseases are partially caused by these chemicals.

During the 1950s large amounts of the pesticide DDT were sprayed all over the United States to kill unwanted insect pests.

Even though American farmers had always produced enough food and there had never been a shortage, the government and the chemical companies still insisted that it was necessary to spray crops with large amounts of chemical pesticides. Carson discovered that in many cases the pesticides did not even destroy all the insect pests they were supposed to. When crops were sprayed with DDT, some bugs died, but others were strong enough to survive. These insects developed a resistance to the pesticides. They multiplied, and soon there was a whole population of insects that DDT could not kill. A new chemical would then have to be sprayed, and then another, over and over again, as the bug killers tried to stay one step ahead of the bugs. All the while new poisons were put into the earth.

Silent Spring pointed out how widespread chemical spraying had become. Millions of square miles in the southern United States had been sprayed with chemicals even more powerful than DDT. It was part of the government's effort to wipe out the fire ant. But fire ants did not eat large amounts of food crops, and except for an occasional bite, they did not bother people very much. In areas where fire ants were sprayed, scientists reported finding dead birds, opossums, and raccoons. There were even cases of farm animals—chickens and cows—becoming sick. The effort to wipe out the fire ant pitted two government agencies against each other. The Department of Agriculture was in favor of chemical spraying. But the Food and Drug Administration, which was receiving complaints from farmers, finally ordered the spraying stopped.

There was no question that in many areas of the world insects destroyed the crops that people depended on for food. Some kind of pest control was needed. Rachel Carson never suggested that all pesticides should be banned; she simply argued for greater control and regulation. She wanted the government to face the problem openly and study whether these chemicals were dangerous to human beings and other animals.

She also advocated using more natural kinds of pest control, such as insect-killing bacteria or insects that eat other insects. The problem with spraying chemicals was that often the "beneficial" insects were killed while the pest insects survived.

Even Rachel Carson did not know of all the dangers caused by these chemicals. Today, for example, it is known that the rains wash poisonous chemicals from the soil into streams and rivers, where eventually they pollute the oceans. Even though she did not write about this problem, Carson would have been the first to recognize how what is done in one place is connected to what happens in another place. "You can't just step in with brute force and change one thing without changing a good many others," she said. To understand what is happening to the environment, she argued, one has to always look at the big picture.

Because of *Silent Spring*, Rachel Carson is now considered a pioneering founder of the ecology movement. This book has inspired millions of Americans to try to live and work in ways that do not hurt the environment. In the words of the editor of *Silent Spring*, Paul Brooks, "She refused to accept the premise that damage to nature was the inevitable cost of progress." Carson was one of the first writers to describe nature not as many, separate living creatures but as a single world of creatures who depend on one another to survive. If one animal disappeared, other animals, even human beings, would be affected. Some scientists had understood this, but Rachel Carson's best-selling book made it possible for millions of ordinary people to understand the dangers of tampering with the natural order.

On April 3, 1963, Rachel Carson was interviewed on
national television by Eric Sevareid and asked about
her fears for the environment.

CHAPTER

6

A Final Victory

It is hard for readers today, with the first Earth Day celebration more than twenty years in the past, to understand just how many people reacted with anger when *Silent Spring* first appeared. It was true that a great many people read and praised her book. Supreme Court justice William O. Douglas called it the "most important chronicle of this century for the human race." President John F. Kennedy had also been moved, and he ordered the government to reexamine its rules on the use of pesticides. But others attacked her viciously. In the light of everything that is now known about the dangers of polluting the environment, these attacks today would probably embarrass the people who made them. All the same, it was a difficult time for Rachel Carson. Her health failing, she still had to defend herself against the most ignorant and unfair statements.

Of course, the chemical companies that made the pesticides were the first to complain. One chemical company sent a letter to the publisher of *Silent Spring*, trying to stop them from publishing the book. The letter suggested that Carson might be a communist. It also made widely exaggerated claims that without chemical pesticides and fertilizers, farmers would not be able to grow enough food and the whole economy would collapse as it did in the Great Depression. Millions of dollars were spent to discredit *Silent Spring* and its author. The chemical industry paid to have pamphlets printed that made fun of Carson's arguments. If Rachel Carson had her way, the pamphlets suggested, insects would inherit the earth. One magazine article said that "her book is more poisonous than the pesticides she condemns." Even the American Medical Association shamelessly attacked her. *Time* magazine called the book an "emotional and inaccurate outburst." *Reader's Digest* canceled its plans to print a short version of the book and instead reprinted the *Time* magazine article criticizing it.

Carson was stung by the unfairness of much of this criticism. Normally a quiet, shy person who did not seek public attention, she decided to go on television to defend her book. On April 3, 1963, the CBS television network broadcast "The Silent Spring of Rachel Carson." The show included interviews with one of Carson's critics, Dr. Robert White-Stevens, who worked for the American Cyanamid Company, as well as Secretary of Agriculture Orville Freeman. But the most important part of the broadcast was the interview with Carson herself, conducted by the respected journalist Eric Sevareid in Carson's home in Maine. Millions of television viewers who had not read *Silent Spring* watched the soft-spoken author carefully present the evidence that pesticides were harmful. "Can anyone believe," she asked Mr. Sevareid and his television audience, "it is possible to lay down such a barrage of poisons on the surface of the earth without making it unfit for all life?" She went on to explain how serious the problem of interfering with nature could be. "We still talk in terms of conquest. We still haven't become mature enough to think of ourselves as only a tiny part of a vast and incredible universe. Man's attitude toward nature is today critically important simply because we have now acquired a fateful power to alter and destroy nature. But man is a part of nature, and his war against nature is inevitably a war against himself."

The television interview made Rachel Carson famous all across America. Because she spoke so well, many of her critics fell silent. Then, on May 15, 1963, the President's Special Advisory Committee issued a report that confirmed many of her arguments against the use of pesticides and toxic chemicals. The report said that "until the publication of *Silent Spring* by Rachel Carson, people were generally unaware of the toxicity of pesticides. The government should present this information to the public in a way that will make it aware of the dangers while recognizing the value of pesticides." Public opinion was now on her side. Magazines that had criticized her changed their opinions. The conservation movement began to grow. In 1964 the U.S. Congress passed a law that forced chemical companies to prove that their products were safe before they could sell them.

Rachel Carson became very popular and received many awards and honors. She had won her battle and made environmentalism something every American could understand and support. But as she said when she became the first woman to be awarded the Audubon Medal, "Conservation is a cause that has no end. There is no point at which we will say 'our work is finished.'"

But at her moment of triumph, Rachel Carson's health began to fail. The cancer inside her was spreading, and she was becoming weaker. She spent much of her time in a wheelchair and often had to cancel public appearances. Because she still loved the sea, she spent as much time as she could at her house on the Maine coast. She made a visit to California, and late in her life, for the first time, she saw the great forests of huge redwoods. She knew that she did not have long to live. After studying some butterflies one morning, she wrote to a friend that "it is a natural and not unhappy thing that a life comes to an end. That is what those brightly fluttering bits of life taught me this morning."

Finally, on April 14, 1964, at the age of fifty-six, Rachel Carson died. Many famous people attended her funeral. England's prince Philip sent a large wreath, and U.S. secretary of the interior Stewart Udall helped carry her coffin to its final resting place. A wildlife refuge was established near her home in Maine and named after her. The government put her picture on a postage stamp. And in 1980, President Jimmy Carter awarded her the Presidential Medal of Freedom. President Carter said of her, "Always concerned, always eloquent, she created a tide of

In 1981 the U.S. government issued a postage stamp with a portrait of Rachel Carson as part of the Postal Service's Great Americans series.

environmental consciousness that has not ebbed."

Rachel Carson is gone, but her books remain alive for new generations of readers. *The Sea Around Us* and *The Edge of the Sea* have shown that both scientific truth and breathtaking beauty can be found in nature. *Silent Spring* made the problem of pollution a national concern, whereas before there were few who even knew

the meaning of ecology. Rachel Carson's gift for language, her honesty and courage, are qualities people will always admire. She understood all this. Just before she died, she had written, "It is good to know that I shall live on even in the minds of many who do not know me and largely through association with things that are beautiful and lovely."

The rocky coast of Maine, Rachel Carson's favorite retreat.

Chronology

1907   Rachel Louise Carson born in Springdale, Pennsylvania, on May 27

1917   United States enters World War I; Rachel's brother joins the U.S. Army Aviation Service

1925–29   Rachel attends Pennsylvania College for Women

1929   Spends summer at Woods Hole Marine Biological Laboratory on Cape Cod; stock market crash ushers in Great Depression

1929–32	Carson attends graduate school at Johns Hopkins; graduates with an M.A. in marine zoology
1935	Father dies; Carson begins writing radio scripts for U.S. Bureau of Fisheries
1936	Employed by the U.S. Bureau of Fisheries as junior aquatic biologist; sister Marian dies
1937	*Atlantic Monthly* publishes "Undersea"
1941	*Under the Sea-Wind* is published; United States enters World War II
1942	Carson appointed assistant to the chief of the office of information at U.S. Fish and Wildlife Service
1949	Named editor in chief of all Fish and Wildlife publications
1950	*The Sea Around Us* is published
1951	*The Sea Around Us* receives the National Book Award
1952	*Under the Sea-Wind* is reissued and joins *The Sea Around Us* on the best-seller list
1955	*The Edge of the Sea* is published
1957	Carson's niece Marjorie dies; Carson adopts Marjorie's son Roger

1958   Mother dies

1960   Carson learns she has breast cancer

1962   *Silent Spring* is published

1963   President's Science Advisory Committee
endorses Carson's views on pesticide use

1964   Carson dies of cancer on April 14

Glossary

atom bomb   a weapon deriving its explosive force from the energy released during the splitting of atomic nuclei

activist   one who takes direct action in support of one side of a controversial issue

aquatic biology   a branch of science dealing with plants and animals that live in water

bacteria   microscopic one-celled organisms

bathysphere   a steel diving sphere used for deep-sea observation

beneficial insects insects that eat other insects and thus act as a natural form of pest control

blast furnace a furnace in which heated compressed air is used to extract metal from ore

biology a branch of science that deals with living organisms

cabinet a body of advisers to the president

cancer a disease in which certain groups of cells begin to multiply in a destructive manner, destroying nearby cells in the process

cold war a term used to describe the shifting struggle for power and prestige between the Western powers and the Communist bloc from the end of World War II until the early 1960s

conservation the planned management of natural resources to prevent exploitation, destruction, or neglect

coral reef limestone formations produced by living organisms; found in shallow, tropical marine waters

DDT a colorless, odorless insecticide toxic to many animals, including humans

dissect to expose the parts, particularly the internal organs, of an animal for scientific examination

ecology   the study of the relationship of organisms to their physical environment and to each other

environment   the physical and chemical factors that act upon an organism or group of organisms and determine its form and survival

environmentalism   the movement to preserve and protect the quality of our natural environment through conservation of natural resources, prevention of pollution, and control of land use

fertilizer   a substance added to soil to replace or increase plant nutrients

Great Depression   in U.S. history, the period of severe economic crises supposedly brought on by the stock market crash of 1929 and lasting into the early 1940s

habitat   the place or type of site where a plant or animal normally grows

key   an island formed of coral

naturalist   someone who studies the development of an organism over time

nuclear weapon   a weapon that gains its destructive energy from the splitting or fusion of atomic nuclei

oceanography   the study of the sea

Pearl Harbor   American naval station in Oahu, Hawaii, that was attacked without warning by the Japanese in December 1941

pesticide   a chemical used to destroy insects harmful to plants or people

pollution   contamination of the environment as a result of the activities of people

primeval   of or relating to the earliest ages of the world

radar   a system that uses radio waves to determine the position, motion, and nature of a remote object

radiation   energy released in the form of waves

slag   the waste left after processing metal

spawning ground   the place where aquatic animals deposit their eggs

suffragettes   in the nineteenth and early twentieth centuries, women who advocated that they should have the right to vote

toxic   poisonous

women's movement   the social movement that began in the nineteenth century and continues today to work for political, social, and educational equality of women and men

zoology   the branch of biology concerned with the study of animal life

Picture Credits

Jake Goldberg is an editor and a freelance writer. He lives in New York City.